EMMANUEL JOSEPH

Divine Blueprint, Aligning Career, Love, and Faith in an AI-Driven World

Copyright © 2025 by Emmanuel Joseph

All rights reserved. No part of this publication may be reproduced, stored or transmitted in any form or by any means, electronic, mechanical, photocopying, recording, scanning, or otherwise without written permission from the publisher. It is illegal to copy this book, post it to a website, or distribute it by any other means without permission.

First edition

*This book was professionally typeset on Reedsy.
Find out more at reedsy.com*

Contents

1	Chapter 1: Embracing the Divine Blueprint	1
2	Chapter 2: Balancing Career and Spirituality	3
3	Chapter 3: Nurturing Relationships in an AI-Driven World	5
4	Chapter 4: Embracing Change and Adaptability	7
5	Chapter 5: Integrating AI and Spirituality	9
6	Chapter 6: Cultivating Mindfulness in the Digital Age	11
7	Chapter 7: Aligning Career with the Divine Blueprint	13
8	Chapter 8: Cultivating Love and Connection	15
9	Chapter 9: Navigating Challenges with Grace and Resilience	17
10	Chapter 10: Embracing Creativity and Innovation	19
11	Chapter 11: The Power of Service and Contribution	21
12	Chapter 12: Cultivating Inner Peace and Well-Being	23
13	Chapter 13: Embracing the Journey of Personal Growth	25
14	Chapter 14: Legacy and Impact: Leaving a Lasting Mark	27
15	Chapter 15: Embracing the Future with Faith and Hope	29
16	Chapter 16: Conclusion: Living in Alignment with the Divine...	31

1

Chapter 1: Embracing the Divine Blueprint

In our rapidly evolving world, the concept of a divine blueprint becomes more relevant than ever. It is the map designed by a higher power, guiding us towards our true purpose in life. Acknowledging and embracing this divine plan requires a deep connection with one's faith, as well as a commitment to listening to the subtle nudges of the universe. This chapter explores the foundational principles of recognizing and aligning with the divine blueprint, highlighting the importance of prayer, meditation, and self-reflection in uncovering one's true path.

Faith serves as the cornerstone for aligning with the divine blueprint. It provides the strength and clarity needed to navigate the complexities of modern life. As artificial intelligence continues to shape our world, faith remains a constant, anchoring us in our values and guiding us towards fulfilling our purpose. The chapter delves into the role of faith in discerning the divine plan, emphasizing the need for trust and surrender to a higher power.

Aligning with the divine blueprint also involves understanding the unique gifts and talents bestowed upon us. Each individual is endowed with specific abilities and passions, which serve as clues to their life's purpose. By recognizing and nurturing these gifts, we can align our career, love, and faith with the divine plan. This chapter encourages readers to embark on a journey of self-discovery, identifying their strengths and passions, and aligning them with their higher purpose.

Finally, the chapter addresses the importance of remaining open to divine guidance. In an AI-driven world, it is easy to become overwhelmed by technology and lose sight of our spiritual connection. By cultivating an awareness of the divine presence in our lives, we can stay attuned to the guidance and wisdom that leads us towards our true purpose. This chapter offers practical tips for maintaining this connection, including setting aside time for daily spiritual practices and surrounding oneself with supportive, like-minded individuals.

2

Chapter 2: Balancing Career and Spirituality

In the fast-paced world of artificial intelligence and rapid technological advancements, finding a balance between career and spirituality can be challenging. This chapter delves into the importance of integrating one's professional life with their spiritual beliefs, creating a harmonious and fulfilling existence. By aligning career choices with the divine blueprint, individuals can experience a sense of purpose and contentment that transcends material success.

One key aspect of balancing career and spirituality is identifying a profession that aligns with one's values and passions. This chapter explores the concept of vocation, encouraging readers to seek out careers that resonate with their higher purpose. By pursuing work that is meaningful and aligned with their spiritual beliefs, individuals can experience a deeper sense of fulfillment and satisfaction. The chapter provides practical advice on how to identify and pursue such careers, emphasizing the importance of introspection and self-awareness.

Another crucial element of balancing career and spirituality is managing stress and maintaining a healthy work-life balance. In an AI-driven world, the pressure to constantly perform and stay ahead can be overwhelming. This chapter offers strategies for managing stress and maintaining a sense of balance, including setting boundaries, prioritizing self-care, and incorporating spiritual practices into daily routines. By creating a balanced and nurturing work environment, individuals can stay connected to their spiritual beliefs and remain aligned with their divine blueprint.

The chapter also addresses the importance of ethical decision-making in the workplace. As technology continues to advance, the ethical implications of AI and other innovations become increasingly significant. This chapter encourages readers to consider the moral and ethical aspects of their professional choices, ensuring that their actions align with their spiritual beliefs and higher purpose. By making conscious, ethical decisions, individuals can contribute to a more just and compassionate world, staying true to their divine blueprint.

3

Chapter 3: Nurturing Relationships in an AI-Driven World

As technology continues to shape our lives, the way we form and maintain relationships also evolves. This chapter explores the challenges and opportunities presented by an AI-driven world, emphasizing the importance of nurturing relationships that align with our divine blueprint. By fostering connections that are rooted in love, trust, and mutual respect, individuals can create a supportive network that enriches their lives and helps them stay true to their higher purpose.

One key aspect of nurturing relationships in an AI-driven world is maintaining genuine, face-to-face connections. While technology offers numerous ways to stay connected, it is essential to prioritize in-person interactions that foster deeper, more meaningful connections. This chapter offers practical advice on how to balance digital communication with face-to-face interactions, ensuring that relationships remain authentic and fulfilling.

Another important element of nurturing relationships is understanding the role of empathy and compassion. In a world increasingly influenced by AI, it is crucial to cultivate these qualities to maintain strong, supportive connections. This chapter delves into the importance of empathy and compassion in relationships, providing tips on how to develop and practice these qualities in daily life. By fostering a sense of understanding and kindness, individuals can create a network of relationships that aligns with their divine blueprint.

The chapter also addresses the impact of AI on romantic relationships. As technology continues to evolve, the way we find and maintain romantic connections also changes. This chapter explores the challenges and opportunities presented by AI in the realm of love, offering insights on how to navigate these changes while staying true to one's higher purpose. By embracing the divine blueprint and remaining open to divine guidance, individuals can cultivate loving, supportive romantic relationships that align with their spiritual beliefs.

Finally, the chapter emphasizes the importance of surrounding oneself with like-minded individuals who share similar values and beliefs. In an AI-driven world, it is essential to create a supportive network that encourages personal growth and spiritual development. This chapter offers practical advice on how to identify and connect with such individuals, fostering relationships that nourish the soul and help individuals stay aligned with their divine blueprint.

4

Chapter 4: Embracing Change and Adaptability

In an AI-driven world, change is constant and adaptability is crucial. This chapter explores the importance of embracing change and developing the skills needed to navigate an ever-evolving landscape. By aligning with the divine blueprint, individuals can cultivate a sense of resilience and flexibility that allows them to thrive in the face of uncertainty.

One key aspect of embracing change is cultivating a growth mindset. This chapter delves into the concept of a growth mindset, encouraging readers to view challenges and setbacks as opportunities for growth and development. By adopting this mindset, individuals can remain open to new experiences and possibilities, staying aligned with their divine blueprint even in the face of change. The chapter provides practical advice on how to develop and maintain a growth mindset, emphasizing the importance of self-awareness and continuous learning.

Another crucial element of adaptability is developing the skills needed to thrive in an AI-driven world. This chapter explores the importance of lifelong learning and skill development, encouraging readers to stay current with technological advancements and industry trends. By continually updating their skills and knowledge, individuals can remain competitive and adaptable, ensuring that they remain aligned with their higher purpose. The chapter offers practical tips on how to identify and pursue relevant learning opportunities, emphasizing the importance of curiosity and a proactive approach to personal development.

The chapter also addresses the importance of resilience in navigating change. In an AI-driven world, the ability to bounce back from setbacks and maintain a positive outlook is essential. This chapter offers strategies for developing resilience, including cultivating a strong support network, practicing self-care, and maintaining a sense of perspective. By building resilience, individuals can remain grounded and focused on their divine blueprint, even in the face of adversity.

Finally, the chapter emphasizes the importance of staying connected to one's spiritual beliefs during times of change. In an ever-evolving world, it is essential to maintain a sense of grounding and connection to a higher power. This chapter offers practical advice on how to incorporate spiritual practices into daily life, ensuring that individuals remain aligned with their divine blueprint and navigate change with grace and wisdom.

5

Chapter 5: Integrating AI and Spirituality

As artificial intelligence continues to shape our world, it is essential to find ways to integrate AI with our spiritual beliefs. This chapter explores the potential for AI to enhance our spiritual lives, offering insights on how to use technology as a tool for personal growth and spiritual development. By aligning AI with the divine blueprint, individuals can create a harmonious relationship between technology and spirituality.

One key aspect of integrating AI and spirituality is using technology to enhance spiritual practices. This chapter delves into the various ways AI can support meditation, prayer, and other spiritual activities, offering practical tips on how to incorporate these tools into daily routines. By leveraging AI to deepen their spiritual connection, individuals can stay aligned with their higher purpose and experience a greater sense of fulfillment.

Another important element of integrating AI and spirituality is exploring the ethical implications of technology. As AI continues to advance, it is crucial to consider the moral and ethical aspects of its development and use. This chapter encourages readers to reflect on the ethical dimensions of AI, ensuring that their actions and choices align with their spiritual beliefs and higher purpose. By making conscious, ethical decisions, individuals can contribute to a more just and compassionate world, staying true to their divine blueprint.

The chapter also addresses the potential for AI to enhance self-awareness and personal growth. By using AI-driven tools for self-reflection and introspection, individuals can gain valuable insights into their thoughts, emotions, and behaviors. This chapter offers practical advice on how to use AI for self-awareness, encouraging readers to embrace technology as a tool for personal development. By integrating AI with their spiritual beliefs, individuals can experience a deeper sense of self-awareness and alignment with their divine blueprint.

Finally, the chapter emphasizes the importance of maintaining a balanced relationship with technology. In an AI-driven world, it is easy to become consumed by technology and lose sight of one's spiritual connection. This chapter offers practical tips on how to create a balanced relationship with AI, ensuring that individuals remain grounded in their spiritual beliefs while leveraging technology for personal growth. By maintaining this balance, individuals can stay aligned with their divine blueprint and navigate the complexities of an AI-driven world with grace and wisdom.

6

Chapter 6: Cultivating Mindfulness in the Digital Age

In an increasingly digital world, cultivating mindfulness is essential for maintaining a sense of balance and well-being. This chapter explores the importance of mindfulness in an AI-driven society, offering practical techniques for staying present and connected to one's spiritual beliefs. By incorporating mindfulness practices into daily life, individuals can remain aligned with their divine blueprint and navigate the complexities of modern life with greater ease.

One key aspect of cultivating mindfulness is developing a daily meditation practice. This chapter delves into the benefits of meditation, emphasizing its role in reducing stress, enhancing self-awareness, and fostering a deeper connection to a higher power. Practical tips and guided exercises are provided to help readers establish and maintain a consistent meditation routine, ensuring that they remain grounded and centered amidst the chaos of the digital age.

Another important element of mindfulness is practicing mindful breathing. This chapter explores the power of conscious breathing in promoting relaxation and mental clarity. By incorporating mindful breathing techniques into their daily routines, individuals can stay present and focused, reducing the impact of digital distractions on their well-being. The chapter offers simple yet effective breathing exercises that can be easily integrated into busy schedules, helping readers cultivate a sense of calm and balance.

The chapter also addresses the role of mindfulness in managing digital overload. In an AI-driven world, it is easy to become overwhelmed by the constant stream of information and notifications. This chapter provides strategies for managing digital distractions and creating healthy boundaries with technology. By practicing mindful consumption of digital media, individuals can maintain a sense of balance and focus, ensuring that they remain aligned with their divine blueprint.

Finally, the chapter emphasizes the importance of incorporating mindfulness into daily activities. By approaching everyday tasks with a sense of presence and intention, individuals can transform mundane routines into opportunities for spiritual growth and self-awareness. This chapter offers practical tips on how to bring mindfulness into daily life, encouraging readers to stay connected to their higher purpose and cultivate a sense of inner peace.

7

Chapter 7: Aligning Career with the Divine Blueprint

Finding a career that aligns with one's divine blueprint is a crucial aspect of living a fulfilling and purposeful life. This chapter explores the process of discerning one's vocation, offering insights and practical advice on how to identify and pursue a career that resonates with one's higher purpose. By aligning their professional lives with their spiritual beliefs, individuals can experience a deeper sense of fulfillment and satisfaction.

One key aspect of aligning career with the divine blueprint is understanding one's unique gifts and talents. This chapter encourages readers to embark on a journey of self-discovery, identifying their strengths, passions, and interests. By recognizing and nurturing these gifts, individuals can find a career that aligns with their higher purpose and contributes to their overall sense of fulfillment. Practical exercises and reflective questions are provided to help readers uncover their true calling.

Another important element of aligning career with the divine blueprint is seeking out work that is meaningful and aligned with one's values. This chapter explores the concept of purposeful work, encouraging readers to pursue careers that make a positive impact on the world and align with their spiritual beliefs. By prioritizing meaning and purpose in their professional lives, individuals can stay true to their divine blueprint and experience a greater sense of satisfaction and fulfillment.

The chapter also addresses the importance of finding a work-life balance that supports one's spiritual growth. In an AI-driven world, it is easy to become consumed by work and lose sight of one's higher purpose. This chapter offers strategies for creating a balanced and nurturing work environment, ensuring that individuals can stay connected to their spiritual beliefs while pursuing their professional goals. Practical tips on setting boundaries, prioritizing self-care, and incorporating spiritual practices into daily routines are provided to help readers maintain a healthy work-life balance.

Finally, the chapter emphasizes the importance of remaining open to divine guidance in one's career journey. By staying attuned to the subtle nudges of the universe, individuals can navigate their professional lives with greater ease and clarity. This chapter offers practical advice on how to cultivate a sense of openness and receptivity to divine guidance, ensuring that readers remain aligned with their divine blueprint and experience a fulfilling and purposeful career.

8

Chapter 8: Cultivating Love and Connection

Love is a fundamental aspect of the divine blueprint, and cultivating meaningful connections is essential for living a fulfilling life. This chapter explores the importance of love and connection in an AI-driven world, offering insights and practical advice on how to nurture relationships that align with one's higher purpose. By fostering connections rooted in love, trust, and mutual respect, individuals can create a supportive network that enriches their lives and helps them stay true to their divine blueprint.

One key aspect of cultivating love and connection is understanding the role of empathy and compassion in relationships. This chapter delves into the importance of these qualities in building strong, supportive connections, providing tips on how to develop and practice empathy and compassion in daily life. By fostering a sense of understanding and kindness, individuals can create relationships that align with their higher purpose and contribute to their overall sense of fulfillment.

Another important element of cultivating love and connection is prioritizing genuine, face-to-face interactions. While technology offers numerous ways to stay connected, it is essential to maintain in-person connections that foster deeper, more meaningful relationships. This chapter offers practical advice on how to balance digital communication with face-to-face interactions, ensuring that relationships remain authentic and fulfilling.

The chapter also addresses the impact of AI on romantic relationships. As technology continues to evolve, the way we find and maintain romantic connections also changes. This chapter explores the challenges and opportunities presented by AI in the realm of love, offering insights on how to navigate these changes while staying true to one's higher purpose. By embracing the divine blueprint and remaining open to divine guidance, individuals can cultivate loving, supportive romantic relationships that align with their spiritual beliefs.

Finally, the chapter emphasizes the importance of surrounding oneself with like-minded individuals who share similar values and beliefs. In an AI-driven world, it is essential to create a supportive network that encourages personal growth and spiritual development. This chapter offers practical advice on how to identify and connect with such individuals, fostering relationships that nourish the soul and help individuals stay aligned with their divine blueprint.

9

Chapter 9: Navigating Challenges with Grace and Resilience

Life is filled with challenges, and navigating them with grace and resilience is essential for staying aligned with the divine blueprint. This chapter explores the importance of developing resilience and maintaining a positive outlook in the face of adversity, offering practical strategies for overcoming obstacles and staying true to one's higher purpose.

One key aspect of navigating challenges with grace and resilience is cultivating a strong support network. This chapter emphasizes the importance of surrounding oneself with supportive, like-minded individuals who can provide encouragement and guidance during difficult times. Practical tips on how to build and maintain such a network are provided, ensuring that readers have the support they need to navigate challenges with grace and resilience.

Another important element of resilience is developing a growth mindset. This chapter delves into the concept of a growth mindset, encouraging readers to view challenges and setbacks as opportunities for growth and development. By adopting this mindset, individuals can remain open to new experiences and possibilities, staying aligned with their divine blueprint even in the face of adversity. Practical advice on how to develop and maintain a growth mindset is provided, emphasizing the importance of self-awareness and continuous learning.

The chapter also addresses the role of faith in navigating challenges. In difficult times, faith can provide the strength and clarity needed to overcome obstacles and stay true to one's higher purpose. This chapter explores the importance of maintaining a strong spiritual connection during times of adversity, offering practical tips on how to incorporate spiritual practices into daily life. By staying connected to their faith, individuals can navigate challenges with greater ease and resilience.

Finally, the chapter emphasizes the importance of self-care in maintaining resilience. In an AI-driven world, the pressure to constantly perform and stay ahead can be overwhelming. This chapter offers strategies for managing stress and maintaining a sense of balance, including setting boundaries, prioritizing self-care, and incorporating mindfulness practices into daily routines. By taking care of their physical, emotional, and spiritual well-being, individuals can build the resilience needed to navigate challenges with grace and remain aligned with their divine blueprint.

10

Chapter 10: Embracing Creativity and Innovation

Creativity and innovation are essential aspects of the divine blueprint, allowing individuals to express their unique gifts and contribute to the betterment of the world. This chapter explores the importance of embracing creativity and innovation in an AI-driven society, offering practical insights on how to cultivate and nurture these qualities in daily life.

One key aspect of embracing creativity is recognizing the unique gifts and talents bestowed upon each individual. This chapter encourages readers to explore their creative potential and express their unique gifts in meaningful ways. Practical exercises and reflective questions are provided to help readers uncover their creative passions and align them with their higher purpose.

Another important element of creativity and innovation is fostering a mindset of curiosity and open-mindedness. This chapter delves into the importance of remaining open to new ideas and experiences, encouraging readers to embrace the unknown and take risks in their creative endeavors. By cultivating a sense of curiosity and open-mindedness, individuals can stay aligned with their divine blueprint and contribute to the betterment of society through their innovative ideas and actions.

The chapter also addresses the role of collaboration in fostering creativity and innovation. In an AI-driven world, the ability to work effectively with others and leverage diverse perspectives is essential for achieving creative breakthroughs. This chapter offers practical advice on how to build and maintain collaborative relationships, ensuring that readers can harness the power of teamwork to bring their creative visions to life.

Finally, the chapter emphasizes the importance of staying connected to one's spiritual beliefs while pursuing creative and innovative endeavors. By aligning their creative expressions with their higher purpose, individuals can experience a deeper sense of fulfillment and contribute to the betterment of the world. Practical tips on how to incorporate spiritual practices into creative routines are provided, ensuring that readers remain grounded and connected to their divine blueprint as they explore their creative potential.

11

Chapter 11: The Power of Service and Contribution

Service and contribution are fundamental aspects of the divine blueprint, allowing individuals to make a positive impact on the world and fulfill their higher purpose. This chapter explores the importance of serving others and contributing to the greater good, offering practical insights on how to align one's actions with their spiritual beliefs and higher purpose.

One key aspect of service and contribution is recognizing the unique ways in which individuals can make a difference. This chapter encourages readers to identify their strengths, talents, and passions, and use them to serve others. By leveraging their unique gifts for the benefit of others, individuals can experience a deeper sense of fulfillment and align their actions with their divine blueprint. Practical exercises and reflective questions are provided to help readers uncover their unique contributions and explore ways to serve their communities.

Another important element of service is developing a mindset of compassion and generosity. This chapter delves into the importance of cultivating a heart of service, encouraging readers to approach every interaction with empathy and kindness. By fostering a spirit of generosity, individuals can make a positive impact on the world and create meaningful connections with others. The chapter offers practical advice on how to develop and practice compassion in daily life, ensuring that readers remain aligned with their higher purpose.

The chapter also addresses the role of service in fostering a sense of community. In an AI-driven world, it is essential to build and maintain strong, supportive communities that encourage personal growth and spiritual development. This chapter explores the importance of creating a sense of belonging and connection through acts of service, offering practical tips on how to engage with and contribute to one's community. By fostering a sense of community, individuals can stay aligned with their divine blueprint and experience a greater sense of fulfillment.

Finally, the chapter emphasizes the importance of staying open to divine guidance in one's service journey. By remaining receptive to the subtle nudges of the universe, individuals can discover new and meaningful ways to serve others. This chapter offers practical advice on how to cultivate a sense of openness and receptivity to divine guidance, ensuring that readers remain aligned with their divine blueprint and make a positive impact on the world through their actions.

12

Chapter 12: Cultivating Inner Peace and Well-Being

Inner peace and well-being are essential for living a fulfilling and purposeful life. This chapter explores the importance of cultivating a sense of inner calm and balance, offering practical techniques for achieving and maintaining well-being in an AI-driven world. By nurturing their mental, emotional, and spiritual health, individuals can stay aligned with their divine blueprint and navigate the complexities of modern life with greater ease.

One key aspect of cultivating inner peace is developing a daily self-care routine. This chapter delves into the importance of prioritizing self-care, offering practical tips on how to create and maintain a nurturing self-care practice. By taking care of their physical, emotional, and spiritual well-being, individuals can build a strong foundation for inner peace and remain aligned with their higher purpose.

Another important element of well-being is managing stress and maintaining a healthy work-life balance. In an AI-driven world, the pressure to constantly perform and stay ahead can be overwhelming. This chapter offers strategies for managing stress and maintaining a sense of balance, including setting boundaries, prioritizing relaxation, and incorporating mindfulness practices into daily routines. By creating a balanced and nurturing environment, individuals can stay connected to their spiritual beliefs and remain aligned with their divine blueprint.

The chapter also addresses the importance of fostering positive relationships and creating a supportive network. By surrounding themselves with like-minded individuals who share similar values and beliefs, individuals can cultivate a sense of connection and support that contributes to their overall well-being. This chapter offers practical advice on how to build and maintain strong, supportive relationships, ensuring that readers have the encouragement and guidance they need to stay aligned with their higher purpose.

Finally, the chapter emphasizes the importance of staying connected to one's spiritual beliefs in achieving inner peace. By incorporating spiritual practices into daily life, individuals can maintain a sense of grounding and connection to a higher power. This chapter offers practical tips on how to cultivate a strong spiritual connection, ensuring that readers remain aligned with their divine blueprint and experience a deeper sense of inner peace and well-being.

13

Chapter 13: Embracing the Journey of Personal Growth

Personal growth is a continuous journey that requires dedication, self-awareness, and a commitment to living in alignment with the divine blueprint. This chapter explores the importance of embracing personal growth and offers practical insights on how to cultivate a mindset of continuous improvement and self-discovery.

One key aspect of personal growth is developing a sense of self-awareness. This chapter encourages readers to engage in regular self-reflection, identifying areas for growth and development. Practical exercises and reflective questions are provided to help readers gain a deeper understanding of themselves and their unique strengths and challenges. By cultivating self-awareness, individuals can stay aligned with their higher purpose and make conscious choices that contribute to their personal growth.

Another important element of personal growth is setting and pursuing meaningful goals. This chapter delves into the importance of goal-setting, offering practical tips on how to identify and achieve goals that align with one's divine blueprint. By setting and pursuing goals that are in harmony with their higher purpose, individuals can experience a greater sense of fulfillment and satisfaction. The chapter provides strategies for setting SMART (Specific, Measurable, Achievable, Relevant, Time-bound) goals, ensuring that readers have a clear roadmap for their personal growth journey.

The chapter also addresses the role of resilience in personal growth. In an AI-driven world, the ability to bounce back from setbacks and maintain a positive outlook is essential for continuous improvement. This chapter offers strategies for developing resilience, including cultivating a growth mindset, building a strong support network, and practicing self-care. By developing resilience, individuals can navigate challenges with grace and remain committed to their personal growth journey.

Finally, the chapter emphasizes the importance of staying open to new experiences and opportunities for growth. By embracing a mindset of curiosity and open-mindedness, individuals can discover new paths and possibilities that contribute to their personal development. This chapter offers practical advice on how to stay open to new experiences, ensuring that readers remain aligned with their divine blueprint and continue to grow and evolve on their personal growth journey.

14

Chapter 14: Legacy and Impact: Leaving a Lasting Mark

The legacy we leave behind is a reflection of how we have lived in alignment with our divine blueprint. This chapter explores the importance of considering the impact of our actions and decisions, offering practical insights on how to leave a positive and lasting legacy.

One key aspect of leaving a lasting legacy is living with intention and purpose. This chapter encourages readers to reflect on their values and beliefs, ensuring that their actions and decisions align with their higher purpose. By living with intention, individuals can create a meaningful impact on the world and leave behind a legacy that reflects their commitment to the divine blueprint. Practical exercises and reflective questions are provided to help readers identify their core values and align their actions with their higher purpose.

Another important element of legacy is contributing to the greater good. This chapter delves into the importance of service and giving back, encouraging readers to use their unique gifts and talents to make a positive impact on the world. By engaging in acts of service and contributing to their communities, individuals can create a lasting legacy that reflects their commitment to living in alignment with their divine blueprint. Practical tips on how to identify and pursue meaningful opportunities for service are provided, ensuring that readers have the tools they need to make a positive impact.

The chapter also addresses the importance of fostering positive relationships and creating a supportive network. By building strong, meaningful connections with others, individuals can create a ripple effect of positive influence that extends beyond their immediate circle. This chapter offers practical advice on how to build and maintain strong relationships, ensuring that readers leave behind a legacy of love, trust, and mutual respect.

Finally, the chapter emphasizes the importance of staying connected to one's spiritual beliefs in considering the impact of one's actions. By incorporating spiritual practices into daily life and remaining attuned to divine guidance, individuals can ensure that their legacy reflects their commitment to the divine blueprint. This chapter offers practical tips on how to cultivate a strong spiritual connection, ensuring that readers leave behind a lasting impact that aligns with their higher purpose.

15

Chapter 15: Embracing the Future with Faith and Hope

As we move into the future, it is essential to remain grounded in our faith and hold onto hope for what lies ahead. This chapter explores the importance of embracing the future with a sense of optimism and trust in the divine blueprint, offering practical insights on how to navigate the uncertainties of an AI-driven world with faith and hope.

One key aspect of embracing the future is cultivating a sense of trust and surrender to a higher power. This chapter encourages readers to place their faith in the divine plan, knowing that they are being guided towards their higher purpose. Practical tips on how to cultivate trust and surrender are provided, ensuring that readers remain grounded in their faith and approach the future with a sense of confidence and optimism.

Another important element of embracing the future is maintaining a positive outlook. This chapter delves into the importance of focusing on the positive aspects of life and maintaining a sense of hope, even in the face of challenges and uncertainties. Practical strategies for cultivating a positive mindset are offered, including practicing gratitude, staying connected to supportive individuals, and engaging in activities that bring joy and fulfillment.

The chapter also addresses the role of adaptability in navigating the future.

In an ever-evolving world, the ability to adapt and remain flexible is essential for staying aligned with the divine blueprint. This chapter offers practical advice on how to develop and maintain adaptability, ensuring that readers can navigate the uncertainties of the future with grace and resilience.

Finally, the chapter emphasizes the importance of staying connected to one's spiritual beliefs as we move into the future. By incorporating spiritual practices into daily life and remaining attuned to divine guidance, individuals can navigate the future with a sense of peace and confidence. This chapter offers practical tips on how to cultivate a strong spiritual connection, ensuring that readers embrace the future with faith and hope, staying true to their divine blueprint.

16

Chapter 16: Conclusion: Living in Alignment with the Divine Blueprint

The journey of aligning career, love, and faith in an AI-driven world is one of continuous self-discovery, growth, and dedication to living in harmony with the divine blueprint. This chapter serves as a conclusion, highlighting the key principles and practices that can help individuals stay true to their higher purpose and navigate the complexities of modern life with grace and wisdom.

One key aspect of living in alignment with the divine blueprint is maintaining a strong spiritual connection. This chapter emphasizes the importance of incorporating spiritual practices into daily life, ensuring that individuals remain grounded and connected to a higher power. Practical tips on how to cultivate a strong spiritual connection are provided, including setting aside time for prayer and meditation, engaging in acts of service, and surrounding oneself with supportive, like-minded individuals.

Another important element of living in alignment with the divine blueprint is embracing change and adaptability. In an ever-evolving world, the ability to adapt and remain flexible is essential for staying true to one's higher purpose. This chapter offers practical advice on how to develop and maintain adaptability, ensuring that readers can navigate the uncertainties of the future with grace and resilience. By embracing change and remaining open to new experiences, individuals can stay aligned with their divine blueprint and continue to grow and evolve on their spiritual journey.

The chapter also addresses the importance of cultivating inner peace and well-being. By prioritizing self-care and managing stress, individuals can build a strong foundation for inner peace and remain aligned with their higher purpose. Practical strategies for achieving and maintaining well-being are provided, ensuring that readers have the tools they need to navigate the complexities of modern life with greater ease.

Finally, the chapter emphasizes the importance of leaving a lasting legacy and making a positive impact on the world. By living with intention and purpose, individuals can create a meaningful impact that reflects their commitment to the divine blueprint. This chapter encourages readers to reflect on their values and beliefs, ensuring that their actions and decisions align with their higher purpose. By living in alignment with the divine blueprint, individuals can experience a deeper sense of fulfillment and contribute to the betterment of the world.

With these principles and practices in mind, readers can embark on a journey of aligning career, love, and faith in an AI-driven world. By staying true to the divine blueprint, individuals can navigate the complexities of modern life with grace, wisdom, and a sense of purpose. May this book serve as a guiding light, inspiring readers to live in harmony with their higher purpose and create a positive impact on the world.

Book Description: Divine Blueprint: Aligning Career, Love, and Faith in an AI-Driven World

In the face of the rapid technological advancements reshaping our world, "Divine Blueprint: Aligning Career, Love, and Faith in an AI-Driven World" offers a beacon of hope and guidance. This transformative book delves into the intricate interplay between spirituality, relationships, and professional life, providing readers with practical insights and strategies to harmonize their existence.

Each chapter unveils a new layer of understanding, from embracing the divine blueprint and balancing career with spirituality, to nurturing meaningful relationships in an AI-driven society. Readers will explore the

CHAPTER 16: CONCLUSION: LIVING IN ALIGNMENT WITH THE DIVINE...

importance of empathy, adaptability, and mindfulness, while discovering ways to integrate technology with their spiritual practices.

Through the lens of personal growth, the book emphasizes resilience, creativity, and ethical decision-making, guiding readers to cultivate inner peace and well-being. The journey culminates in a powerful reflection on legacy and impact, inspiring individuals to live with intention and purpose.

With a unique blend of spiritual wisdom and practical advice, "Divine Blueprint" empowers readers to navigate the complexities of modern life, fostering a sense of fulfillment and alignment with their higher purpose. Whether you're seeking to deepen your faith, enhance your relationships, or find your true calling, this book offers a roadmap to a harmonious and meaningful life in an AI-driven world.

www.ingramcontent.com/pod-product-compliance
Lightning Source LLC
LaVergne TN
LVHW020500080526
838202LV00057B/6070